Tools

Search

Notes
Discuss

MyReportLinks.com Books

Go!

## PRESIDENTS

# ZACHARY TAYLOR

## A MyReportLinks.com Book

James Deem

# MyReportLinks.com Books

an imprint of

**Enslow Publishers, Inc.** E

Box 398, 40 Industrial Road
Berkeley Heights, NJ 07922
USA

MyReportLinks.com Books, an imprint of Enslow Publishers, Inc.

**Library of Congress Cataloging-in-Publication Data**

Deem, James M.
   Zachary Taylor: a MyReportLinks.com book / James Deem.
     p. cm. — (Presidents)
     Includes bibliographical references and index.
  Summary: Traces the life of the twelfth president of the United States, who rose to
prominence from a distinguished military career. Includes Internet links to Web sites,
source documents, and photographs related to Zachary Taylor.
     ISBN 0-7660-5013-0
     1. Taylor, Zachary, 1784–1850—Juvenile literature. 2. Presidents—United States—
Biography—Juvenile literature. [1. Taylor, Zachary, 1784–1850. 2. Presidents.] I. Title. II.
Series.

E422 .D44 2002
973.6'3'092—dc21
[B]

2001004308


Printed in the United States of America

10 9 8 7 6 5 4 3 2 1

**To Our Readers:** We have done our best to make sure all Internet addresses in this book
were active and appropriate when we went to press. However, the author and the Publisher
have no control over, and assume no liability for, the material available on those Internet
sites or on other Web sites they may link to. The Publisher will try to keep the Report Links
that back up this book up to date on our Web site for three years from the book's
first publication date. Any comments or suggestions can be sent by e-mail to
comments@myreportlinks.com or to the address on the back cover.

**Photo Credits:** © Corel Corporation, pp. 1 (background), 3; Courtesy of
America's Library, pp. 31, 33, 34; Courtesy of American Memory/Library of
Congress, pp. 24, 38; Courtesy of Black Hawk War of 1832, p. 21; Courtesy of
Descendants of Mexican War Veterans, pp. 13, 26, 28, 29, 30; Courtesy of
MyReportLinks.com Books, p. 4; Courtesy of National Portrait Gallery,
Smithsonian Institution, p. 43; Courtesy of Papers of Jefferson Davis: Jefferson
Davis FAQs, p. 22; Courtesy of PBS, p. 32; *Dictionary of American Portraits,*
Dover Publications, Inc., © 1967, pp. 1, 11, 18, 40; Library of Congress, pp. 16,
26, 35, 36; *Old West Cuts,* © 1995 Dover Publications, Inc., p. 14.

**Cover Photos:** © Corel Corporation (background); National Portrait Gallery,
Smithsonian Institution, gift of Barry Bingham, Sr.

# Contents

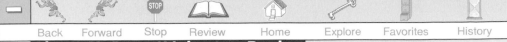
# MyReportLinks.com Books
## Great Books, Great Links, Great for Research!

MyReportLinks.com Books present the information you need to learn about your report subject. In addition, they show you where to go on the Internet for more information. The pre-evaluated Report Links, listed on **www.myreportlinks.com**, save hours of research time and link to dozens—even hundreds—of Web sites, source documents, and photos related to your report topic.

**To Our Readers:**

Each Report Link has been reviewed by our editors, who will work hard to keep only active and appropriate Internet addresses in our books and up to date on our Web site. However, the author and the Publisher have no control over, and assume no liability for, the material available on those Internet sites, or on other Web sites they may link to.

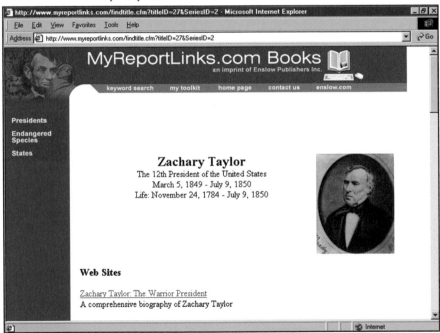

**Access:**

The Publisher will try to keep the Report Links that back up this book up to date on our Web site for three years from the book's first publication date. Please enter **PTA13U7** if asked for a password.

## Report Links

 The Internet sites described below can be accessed at
**http://www.myreportlinks.com**

*EDITOR'S CHOICE

▶**Zachary Taylor: The Warrior President**
This site provides a comprehensive biography of Zachary Taylor's life
before, during, and after his presidency.

Link to this Internet site from http://www.myreportlinks.com

*EDITOR'S CHOICE

▶**The American Presidency: Zachary Taylor**
At this site you will find Zachary Taylor's inaugural address, quick
facts, and a detailed biography.

Link to this Internet site from http://www.myreportlinks.com

*EDITOR'S CHOICE

▶**Zachary Taylor**
This site contains facts and figures on Zachary Taylor. You will also
find links to election results, cabinet members, notable events,
biographies, and historical documents.

Link to this Internet site from http://www.myreportlinks.com

*EDITOR'S CHOICE

▶**"I Do Solemnly Swear..."**
Get a firsthand look at Zachary Taylor's Inauguration Day through
images and documents.

Link to this Internet site from http://www.myreportlinks.com

*EDITOR'S CHOICE

▶**Zachary Taylor**
The official White House Web site holds the biography of
Zachary Taylor.

Link to this Internet site from http://www.myreportlinks.com

*EDITOR'S CHOICE

▶**The U.S.-Mexican War 1846–1848**
This comprehensive site tells the story of the Mexican War. Here you
will find images, maps, and historical documents related to the war.

Link to this Internet site from http://www.myreportlinks.com

Any comments? Contact us: **comments@myreportlinks.com**    5

The Internet sites described below can be accessed at
**http://www.myreportlinks.com**

▶**American Presidents: Zachary Taylor**
At this site you will find basic facts about Zachary Taylor and a letter written
by him.

Link to this Internet site from http://www.myreportlinks.com

▶**Antonio López de Santa Anna: A Man and His Times**
At this site Santa Anna's character is analyzed completely. Here you will learn
what motivated him, and how he was viewed by Mexico and other nations.

Link to this Internet site from http://www.myreportlinks.com

▶**The Battle of Buena Vista**
Zachary Taylor's victories in the Mexican War gave way to his election
in 1848.

Link to this Internet site from http://www.myreportlinks.com

▶**Black Hawk War of 1832**
This site contains a brief, yet concise, history of the Black Hawk War and the
men who fought in it. You will also find maps and images relating to the war.

Link to this Internet site from http://www.myreportlinks.com

▶**Clayton-Bulwer Treaty**
At this site you will find the text of the Clayton-Bulwer Treaty.

Link to this Internet site from http://www.myreportlinks.com

▶**Gold Fever**
Take a virtual tour of the Gold Rush and learn about the people involved.

Link to this Internet site from http://www.myreportlinks.com

## Report Links

 The Internet sites described below can be accessed at
**http://www.myreportlinks.com**

▶ **Margaret Smith Mackall Taylor**
The official White House Web site holds the biography of Margaret Smith Mackall Taylor. Here you will learn how Mackall met Taylor, and about their life in the White House.

Link to this Internet site from http://www.myreportlinks.com

▶ **Millard Fillmore**
This site contains a brief biography of Millard Fillmore, Taylor's vice president. Learn how Fillmore was able to sign into law the much debated Compromise of 1850.

Link to this Internet site from http://www.myreportlinks.com

▶ **The National Park Service: Palo Alto Battlefield National Historic Site**
The National Park Service Web site provides a brief history of the Battle of Palo Alto.

Link to this Internet site from http://www.myreportlinks.com

▶ **National Register of Historic Places Travel Itinerary: Florida: Zachary Taylor**
This site provides a map of Zachary Taylor's fort. By clicking on the numbers, you will find a brief description of Taylor's fort, as well as descriptions of other Florida forts.

Link to this Internet site from http://www.myreportlinks.com

▶ **Objects from the Presidency**
At this site you will find information on all the presidents of the United States, including Zachary Taylor. Read a brief description of the era he lived in and learn about the office of the presidency.

Link to this Internet site from http://www.myreportlinks.com

▶ **President Zachary Taylor**
This site contains a brief biography about Zachary Taylor, a quotation, an interesting fact, and a link to his inaugural address. You will also find a list of major events in his administration and a list of his cabinet and supreme court members.

Link to this Internet site from http://www.myreportlinks.com

**Report Links**

### Sarah Knox Taylor Davis

This site describes the courtship between Sarah Knox Taylor Davis and Jefferson Davis. Although Zachary Taylor did not approve of their relationship, Sarah and Jefferson remained in contact and eventually wed.

Link to this Internet site from http://www.myreportlinks.com

### A Shifting Political Landscape

This site provides a brief history of westward expansion. Here you will find descriptions of the Missouri Compromise of 1820, the Compromise of 1850, and the Kansas-Nebraska Act of 1854. You will also find colorful maps revealing the free states and slave states.

Link to this Internet site from http://www.myreportlinks.com

### Taylor, Zachary

This site provides the details of Zachary Taylor's early life, military career, and presidency.

Link to this Internet site from http://www.myreportlinks.com

### The Treaty of Guadalupe Hidalgo

This site describes the events leading up to the Treaty of Guadalupe Hidalgo, which brought an end to the Mexican War. You will also find maps used for the negotiations and the text of the treaty.

Link to this Internet site from http://www.myreportlinks.com

### U.S. Mexican War 1846–1848

This site provides a wealth of information on the Mexican War, including dialogues, time lines, discussions, and resources.

Link to this Internet site from http://www.myreportlinks.com

### Victory at Palo Alto

This site provides a brief description of the two day battle at Palo Alto, and Zachary Taylor's involvement.

Link to this Internet site from http://www.myreportlinks.com

**Report Links**

The Internet sites described below can be accessed at
**http://www.myreportlinks.com**

▶**War of 1812–1814**
Zachary Taylor became a national figure after his courageous defense of
Fort Harrison during the War of 1812.

Link to this Internet site from http://www.myreportlinks.com

▶**Zachary Taylor**
This site offers a small but fascinating collection of trivia about
Zachary Taylor.

Link to this Internet site from http://www.myreportlinks.com

▶**Zachary Taylor**
At this site you will find three images of Zachary Taylor and brief
descriptions of the images.

Link to this Internet site from http://www.myreportlinks.com

▶**Zachary Taylor: The Brunt of Reluctance**
This site is dedicated to presidents thought to have had "An
Independent Cast of Mind." Here you will find a brief description of
Zachary Taylor's character, a historical document, and a video clip.

Link to this Internet site from http://www.myreportlinks.com

▶**Zachary Taylor House Site**
This site describes Zachary Taylor's house in Baton Rouge.

Link to this Internet site from http://www.myreportlinks.com

▶**Zachary Taylor: Inaugural Address**
Bartelby's vast collection of online documents contains Zachary Taylor's
inaugural address, which he delivered on Monday, March 5, 1849.

Link to this Internet site from http://www.myreportlinks.com

## Highlights

**1784**—*Nov. 24:* Zachary Taylor is born in Orange County, Virginia.

**1808**—Commissioned first lieutenant, United States Army.

**1810**—*June 21:* Marries Margaret Mackall Smith.

—Promoted to army captain.

**1811**—Daughter Ann Mackall Taylor is born.

**1812**—Defends Fort Harrison, Indiana Territory.

—Promoted to brevet major.

**1814**—Daughter Sarah Knox Taylor is born.

**1816**—Daughter Octavia Pannill Taylor is born.

**1819**—Daughter Margaret Smith Taylor is born.

**1820**—Daughters Octavia Pannill Taylor and Margaret Smith Taylor die.

**1824**—Daughter Mary Elizabeth Taylor is born.

**1826**—Son Richard Taylor is born.

**1832**—Promoted from lieutenant colonel to colonel.

—Participates in the Black Hawk War.

**1835**—Daughter Sarah Knox Taylor marries Jefferson Davis; dies three months later.

**1837**—Participates in Second Seminole War; wins the Battle of Okeechobee.

**1838**—Promoted to brevet brigadier general and assumes command of troops in Florida Territory.

**1842**—Pays $95,000 for Cypress Grove Plantation in Jefferson County, Mississippi, and its eighty-one slaves.

**1845**—Establishes the "army of occupation" at Corpus Christi, Texas.

**1846**—Defeats Mexican troops; promoted to major general.

**1847**—Defeats Mexican general Santa Anna in the battle of Buena Vista (near Saltillo, Mexico); given a hero's welcome in New Orleans.

**1848**—*June 9:* Becomes the presidential nominee of the Whig party.

—*Nov. 7:* Defeats Lewis Cass and Martin Van Buren to become the twelfth president of the United States. Millard Fillmore is vice president.

**1849**—*March 5:* Presidential Inauguration.

**1850**—Opposes the Compromise of 1850.

—*July 5:* Signs Clayton-Bulwer Treaty.

—*July 9:* Dies after sixteen months in office from illnesses stemming from food poisoning. Fillmore becomes the thirteenth president.

**Chapter 1 ▶**

# Old Rough and Ready, September 1812

The attack began with a series of turkey calls. It was September 3, 1812, and everyone inside Fort Harrison (near present-day Terre Haute, Indiana) knew that there were not any gobbling turkeys in the woods of that area. Those were American Indians calling, and it sounded like trouble. Two brothers volunteered to investigate. They disappeared into the woods. Soon four shots rang out. The brothers' bodies were discovered the next morning.[1]

Things looked bleak for Fort Harrison. The War of 1812 was in its early months. A coalition of American Indian nations, under the leadership of Tecumseh, had been encouraged and armed by the British to attack American settlers in the Northwest Territory. Three forts had already fallen: Mackinac and Detroit had surrendered, while the troops at Fort Dearborn had been massacred. Only three forts remained to protect the pioneers: Fort Madison (in what is now Iowa), Fort Wayne (in present-day Indiana), and Fort Harrison. All three were chosen for

*Shawnee Chief Tecumseh ▶ led a coalition of American Indian nations during the War of 1812.*

attacks that would coincide with the full moon of September 1812.

Fort Harrison was an easy target. Set on a bluff above the Wabash River, it was right in the middle of Indian country. The woods surrounding the fort were full of American Indians. There were perhaps 450 of them, from the Delaware, Potawatomi, Kickapoo, and Miami tribes. They were led by Lalawethika, commonly known as The Prophet, the brother of the great leader Tecumseh.

The fort was also poorly defended. It had only a wooden fence around three sides of its perimeter. Although it had a garrison of fifty men, thirty-four were so sick with fever that they were under a doctor's care. Fort Harrison still had one important advantage: its commander, Captain Zachary Taylor.

On September 4, a group of American Indians led by Chief Lenar approached the gate bearing a white flag. They needed food, the chief announced. He said he would send a representative to the fort the next day to make a more formal request. Taylor sized up the situation. He did not believe the messengers for a moment. Although he had only sixteen healthy men, and Taylor himself was running a fever, he placed the fort on high alert. Even the sick troops were roused to serve.

That night Taylor stationed extra lookouts. At about eleven o'clock the garrison awoke to gunshots. One block-house—a structure for military defense—had been set afire. Whiskey stored inside it ignited and exploded. The fire quickly spread to the attached barracks. To make matters worse, two of Taylor's best fighters decided to jump the wall and make a run for it.

". . . Most of the men immediately gave themselves up for lost," Taylor wrote later, "and I had the greatest difficulty in getting my orders executed . . . from the raging of the fire, the yelling and howling of several hundred Indians, the cries of nine women and children . . ."[2]

Taylor rallied both his troops and the civilians. He ordered the women to fetch water from the well to douse the flames. He commanded some of the men to climb atop the barracks' roof to remove any burning shingles. Protected by the rest of the troops, they succeeded in stopping the fire.

A twenty-foot gap had been burned out of the fence. With the battle still raging, Taylor directed his men to fill

For his bravery and military skill in the War of 1812 and the Mexican War, Congress awarded Taylor with the highest honor by giving him the title of full major general.

▲ *The Prophet.*

the opening with anything they could find. By six o'clock the next morning, after seven hours of fighting, the battle was over. Taylor had lost two men, but the fort was saved.

Once word of the battle spread, Taylor received an honorary promotion to major for his bravery and leadership in the face of such danger. When The Prophet's men could have overrun the fort, Taylor showed determination and bravery in giving orders and sticking to them. These traits served him so well that one day he would be nicknamed Old Rough and Ready.

## Chapter 2

# Taylor's Early Years, 1784–1815

**O**ne day in the fall of 1784, Richard and Sarah Strother Taylor took their two young sons and their belongings and headed west. They left behind their home in eastern Virginia and were traveling to a wilderness called Kentucky. Mrs. Taylor was pregnant at the time. At the end of the first day's twelve-mile journey, they stopped at the home of a relative near Barboursville, Virginia. Sarah remained there with her sons while her husband went on to Kentucky alone and built a log house for the family.

## ▶ Born in Virginia, Raised in Kentucky

Zachary Taylor was born on November 24, 1784. In the spring, his father returned and took his family on horse-back to Redstone Creek in Pennsylvania. There they floated downstream on a flatboat to the Ohio River and a swampy young town known as Louisville, Kentucky.

Zachary grew up in an isolated home that the Taylors named Springfield on the Muddy Fork of Beargrass Creek. Wolves howled at night, and sometimes American Indians skirmished with the local settlers. One of Zachary's teachers, Mr. Whetsel, was said to have battled three or four Indians once.

No one knows if Zachary spent much time thinking about the wilderness or wars with American Indians. Little is known about his childhood at all. He had some formal education from tutors, but his spelling, grammar, and handwriting skills were considered weak. He believed in the importance and value of education, though. Later he

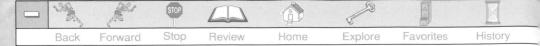
made sure that his own children were well educated. His daughters attended the best private schools. His son was educated in Europe and graduated from Yale.

## Early Commands

Like his father, who was an officer in the Revolutionary War, Zachary enlisted in the military as a young man. In May 1808, Zachary Taylor became a first lieutenant in the Seventh Infantry. He accepted the appointment in this letter, which reflects his struggles with spelling (notice the italicized words) and grammar:

> Sir
>
> I received your letter of the 4th of May in which you informed me that I was appointed a *firs* Lieutenant in the seventh regiment of Infantry in the service of the United States which appointment I *doo* accept.
>
> I am Sir with great respect your able servt,
>
> Zachary Taylor[1]

A month later Indians attacked Fort Pickering (near present-day Memphis, Tennessee) and killed Zachary's older brother William, who had also entered the Army. Although the details were not recorded, Zachary may have been surprised when one of his first military assignments was to command Fort Pickering only a year after his brother's death. His command there, however, lasted only a few uneventful months.

Soon after he left Fort Pickering, Zachary met Margaret Mackall Smith. Her father had been a wealthy planter from Maryland. On June 21, 1810, after a short courtship,

*Zachary Taylor.*

they were married. Taylor was twenty-five years old. His father gave them 324 acres of farmland as a wedding present. Today that land is part of downtown Louisville, Kentucky.

Taylor earned some money as a surveyor; that is, as a person who measures the boundaries of people's land. With that income and a raise in pay from the military he was able to purchase his first two slaves. Over his lifetime he would own 145 slaves.[2]

## A Lack of Recognition

Taylor's next important command came at the start of the War of 1812, when he was assigned to Fort Harrison. Although he had saved the fort from American Indian attacks and was given the honorary promotion, he was not always happy with the recognition he received for his military service.

There were two types of promotion: brevet (honorary) and lineal (actual). His new rank as brevet major was prestigious, but it came without any increase in salary. It bothered Taylor that many other captains had been promoted to a lineal rank of major during his almost two years of service.

Finally, on May 15, 1814, Taylor was promoted to a lineal rank of major, but he never took command of his new unit. The War of 1812 ended in 1815, when Britain and the United States signed the Treaty of Ghent. Now that the war was over, the United States no longer needed a large army. As a consequence, fewer officers were required. On May 3, 1815, Congress acted to reduce the Army from sixty thousand men to ten thousand. Taylor was told that his rank had been reduced to captain again. His pride was hurt. On June 9, 1815, Taylor resigned from military service. He intended to become a full-time farmer.

**Chapter 3 ▶**

# Distinguished Soldier, 1816–1840

**Z**achary Taylor may have been disappointed with his reduction in rank, but he accepted his new role as a farmer without hesitation. He wrote his cousin, "I can assure [you] I do not [regret] the change of calling or the course I have pursued."[1]

Nor did he hesitate to rejoin the military when he was offered a promotion to major the following year. From 1816 to 1840, Taylor distinguished himself as a soldier and rose through the ranks.

## ▶ Promotion and Tragedy

In November 1816, Taylor arrived at Fort Howard at Green Bay on Lake Michigan to assume command. The fort was half finished. Taylor made sure that it was full of creature comforts rare for such an isolated post. Maybe he hoped that his wife and family would join him at the fort, though there is no record that they ever did. Still, his quarters were outfitted with mahogany furniture and good china sent from Louisville.

Taylor was promoted to lieutenant colonel and transferred to the Eighth Infantry in Louisiana in February 1820. By then, he and his wife, Margaret, had four

◀ *Zachary Taylor's wife Margaret.*

daughters. He ferried his family to Bayou Sara, the home of his wife's sister, so that he could spend more time with them. But what should have been a happy time was not. Within five months his daughter Octavia contracted what is thought to have been malaria, which was then called "a violent bilious fever," and died. She was three years old.

Taylor left his command and headed for Bayou Sara to comfort his family. In September his wife fell ill, too. In October his youngest daughter, Margaret, also caught malaria and died. His wife managed to recover, though her health was never the same.

These painful family tragedies caused Taylor to make a decision. Though he had been planning to buy a plantation in Louisiana, the deaths "Almost determined me from even thinking of settling permanently in this country, and it is more than likely when I quit the army, that I shall return to Kentucky."[2] However, he decided to buy a plantation as an investment. In January 1823, Taylor purchased a Louisiana cotton plantation, and he put his cousin in charge. He also brought twenty-two slaves from his Kentucky property to work the land.[3]

## A Family Wedding

From 1821 to 1828 Taylor held various military positions in Cincinnati, Louisville, Washington, and Baton Rouge. During this time his family returned to their home in Kentucky.

When Taylor was assigned to be the commander of Fort Snelling (in present-day Minnesota), he arrived accompanied by his wife and older daughters. The Taylor family had a happy, social time at Fort Snelling. They entertained frequently at dinner parties. His oldest daughter, seventeen-year-old Ann, received a great deal of attention

from the troops. She fell in love with the fort's assistant surgeon, Robert Wood.

When Taylor was transferred to the command of Fort Crawford (in Wisconsin), Dr. Wood married Ann there. Taylor reportedly made certain that the library at Fort Crawford had a wide assortment of history books and newspapers. He also encouraged the establishment of a school for the Winnebago Indians, built in Iowa. It had been promised as part of a treaty with the tribe.

## ▶ The Black Hawk War

In April 1832, Taylor was promoted to colonel and faced the challenges of the Black Hawk War.

The previous spring, a Sauk warrior named Black Hawk was upset that his tribe had sold their land (in what is now Illinois) to the United States government. Black Hawk led about three hundred Sauk Indians back to their old land. They were stopped on the western side of the Mississippi River by the U.S. Army and told to remain there. Around the time Taylor was promoted to colonel, Black Hawk and his followers crossed the Mississippi and headed through Illinois's Rock River Valley. Black Hawk and the Army came to blows, and the Sauk were outnumbered. Many of Black Hawk's people, including women and children, were killed. Black Hawk himself was captured.

Although Taylor's role in the battle was minor, he ordered a lieutenant named Jefferson Davis to escort Black Hawk to the barracks in Rock Island, Illinois. Davis went on to play a more important part in Taylor's life, as well as in the history of the United States.

## ▶ A Father's Loss

While he served under Taylor's command, Jefferson Davis developed an attraction to eighteen-year-old Sarah Knox

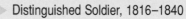
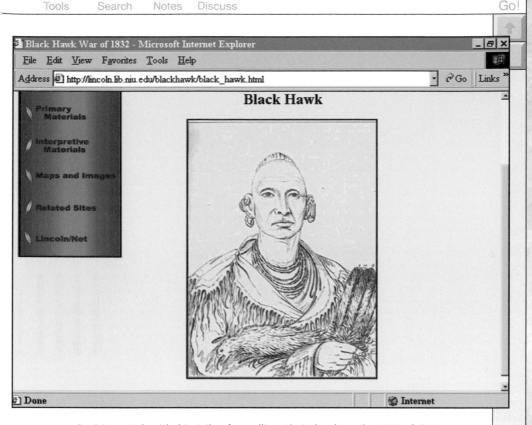

Black Hawk War of 1832 - Microsoft Internet Explorer

File   Edit   View   Favorites   Tools   Help

Address http://lincoln.lib.niu.edu/blackhawk/black_hawk.html          Go   Links

## Black Hawk

Done                                                    Internet

▲ *Disgusted with his tribe for selling their land to the United States government, Black Hawk led a troop of three hundred Sauk Indians back to their land.*

Taylor, Taylor's second oldest daughter. Four years out of West Point, Davis might have been considered a good choice for a son-in-law, but Taylor did not think so.

"I will be damned if another daughter of mine shall marry into the Army," he stated to another officer. "I know enough of the family life of officers. I scarcely know my own children or they me."[4] He was troubled by the sacrifices his wife had made while he was in the military and the hardships his oldest daughter Ann had endured after she married an Army doctor.

Though Taylor stated that he had no personal objections to Davis, he soon would. Davis was reassigned to

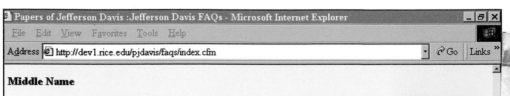

Papers of Jefferson Davis :Jefferson Davis FAQs - Microsoft Internet Explorer

File  Edit  View  Favorites  Tools  Help

Address http://dev1.rice.edu/pjdavis/faqs/index.cfm | Go | Links »

### Middle Name

From November 30, 1824, until mid-1833, Jefferson Davis' name on official lists and at times his signature included the middle initial "F." The name is not spelled out in full in any known document. In his story of Davis' life, Hudson Strode claimed that the final son born to Samuel and Jane Davis was given the middle name "Finis" because "it seemed unlikely that Jane Davis would ever bear another child" (*Jefferson Davis: American Patriot*, p. 3). The "Finis" myth has been repeated so often that it has become accepted as fact by many scholarly resources, but there is no evidence for it. All of Jefferson Davis' siblings had traditional names (see Genealogy of the Davis Family).

Perhaps equally curious is the sudden appearance and just as sudden disappearance of the middle initial. Davis had been at West Point for at least three months before it showed up for the first time, on a monthly conduct report. The last known "J. F. Davis" signature is on a note of October 3, 1832, notifying his commanding officer of his acceptance of a furlough. As of the publication of Davis' appointment as second lieutenant of Dragoons on May 4, 1833, the "F." had disappeared from official documents as well. At the time the initial was in use, there were no other Davis officers with the given name Jefferson (Jefferson C. Davis, a Union general in the Civil War, did not enlist until 1846), so it is unlikely the young cadet was trying to avoid mistaken identity. Only two other officers named Davis with the first initial "J." were in the army from 1824-1833, and one of them died in 1828. It should be noted that the "F." was used on Davis' first marriage license (June 17, 1835), although he signed the document without the "F." The initial was not used on his second marriage license ten years later.

Jefferson Davis' signature and the listing of his name on official documents may be traced in the first volume of *The Papers of Jefferson Davis*, which includes all known documents from Davis' birth through 1840 (see Published

Internet

▲ *Taylor's daughter Sarah married Jefferson Davis, who eventually became the first and only president of the Confederacy.*

Kentucky. For two years Davis and Sarah Knox Taylor wrote letters to each other and occasionally met. Finally they were engaged and then married. Zachary Taylor resigned himself to the marriage and gave the newlyweds a generous monetary gift once Davis resigned from the Army.

Jefferson and Sarah Davis moved to Davis's plantation on an island in the Mississippi River, twenty miles south of Vicksburg. Margaret Taylor wrote to her daughter, voicing her concerns about her health. Perhaps she was thinking of her own bout with fever and the deaths of her two daughters. She knew the plantation was in the "fever district."

"Do not make yourself uneasy about me; the country is quite healthy," Sarah Davis replied to her mother.[5]

Still, the newlyweds contracted malaria. Three months after she was married, Sarah Davis died. Jefferson Davis eventually recovered. The tragedy was so painful to Zachary Taylor that it was many years before he spoke to Davis again.

## In the Florida Swamps

In 1837, Taylor participated in the Second Seminole War, which was fought in Florida. Because settlers wanted to expand their control of the Florida Territory, the Florida Seminole Indians were slated for relocation to the west. Many of them, however, wanted to remain on their land.

Soon after Taylor arrived in Florida, one renegade chief named Alligator and his followers lured Taylor and his troops into a cypress swamp. On December 25, 1837, Taylor fought the Battle of Lake Okeechobee, considered the largest battle of the seven-year Second Seminole War. It was also among the bloodiest battles with American Indians during the 1800s.[6]

Taylor commanded two types of soldiers that day: poorly trained civilian volunteers from Missouri, and well-trained members of the First, Fourth, and Sixth Infantry regiments. He ordered the volunteers to advance upon the Seminole position and directed the infantry to hold back. If the volunteers met a strong resistance, they were to fall back, where they would be joined by the infantry.

The Seminoles had taken a strong position on a ridge covered with trees and tall grass that was surrounded by almost a mile of knee-deep swamp. The Missouri volunteers came under heavy fire. When their commander was killed, they retreated in fear. This left the fighting to the infantries.

After a three-hour battle the Seminole were routed. Taylor's men had suffered great losses: twenty-six dead and 112 wounded. All but one of his officers were killed or wounded. "I experienced one of the most trying scenes of my life," he wrote a week after the battle. "The victory was dearly purchased, but I flatter myself that the result will be equivalent to the sacrifice made."[7]

The army's final report on the Seminole War stated that the Battle of Lake Okeechobee was "one of the best fought battles known in our history."[8] James K. Polk and the commanding general praised Taylor. He was awarded the rank of brevet brigadier general, a rare and important honor. It was an unexpected and treasured surprise. Finally,

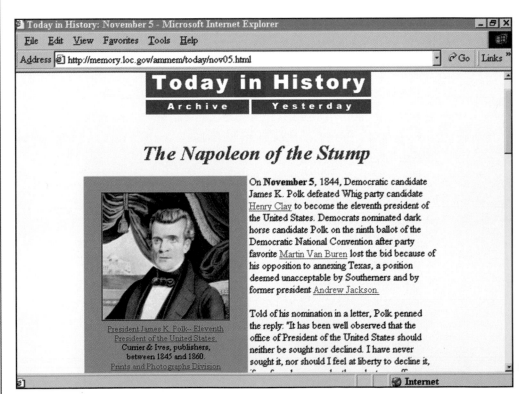

▲ President James K. Polk both praised and criticized Zachary Taylor for his military judgments and tactics.

Taylor assumed command of the Army of the South (that is, all the troops in Florida).

For the next two years, Taylor fought the Seminoles and other American Indians who had fought against Florida's European settlers. The battles were often unsuccessful, because the American Indians lived in small groups. It was easy for them to hide and move undetected to a new site when troops came for them. They desperately wished to stay in their homeland no matter how strong of a force was going to try to remove them.

Taylor became frustrated. His efforts were hampered by a short supply of officers. He even tried to track the native peoples by using an unusual and controversial method: bloodhounds. The dogs, however, were not useful.

## Old Rough and Ready

By early 1840, Taylor had become tired of fighting the American Indian tribes. He asked for reassignment to another state. By this time he had earned a nickname; he was known to the troops who respected him as "Old Rough and Ready."

He earned the name for a couple of reasons. First, he looked like an ordinary man, rough around the edges, not like a commanding officer. In fact, he almost never wore an officer's uniform. A lieutenant once described him this way: "Taylor is short and very heavy . . . wears an old oil cloth cap, a dusty green coat, a frightful pair of trousers and on horseback looks like a toad."[9] His men knew he was approachable and concerned. Second, he fought alongside his soldiers, ready to put himself in great danger. They could not have asked for more in a commanding officer.

To them, Taylor was "Old Rough and Ready." Soon the entire nation would know him by that nickname.

## Chapter 4

# Soldier Turned Politician, 1840–1848

In 1841, Taylor took command of Fort Gibson (near present-day Muskogee, Oklahoma). It was shabby and had the reputation of being the unhealthiest base in the army. Its wood buildings and fences were rotting from the dampness. Although Taylor tried to make the best of the situation by recommending that the Army rebuild the fort, his suggestion was turned down.

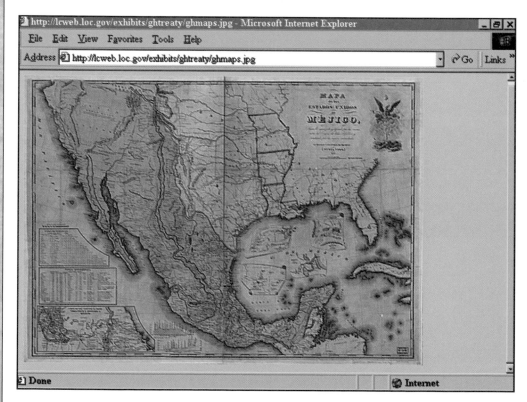

http://lcweb.loc.gov/exhibits/ghtreaty/ghmaps.jpg - Microsoft Internet Explorer

File  Edit  View  Favorites  Tools  Help

Address http://lcweb.loc.gov/exhibits/ghtreaty/ghmaps.jpg  Go  Links

Done  Internet

▲ This map of Mexico and Texas was used for the negotiations for the Treaty of Guadalupe Hidalgo.

He moved his headquarters near Fort Smith, Arkansas, and demonstrated his leadership ability over the next three years. He kept peace with the Cherokee, Creek, and Seminole Indians. He also did the surveying for the construction of Fort Washita in present-day Oklahoma, in order to abandon another fort because it was located in the middle of important Cherokee lands. Although many white settlers protested, Taylor fought for his belief. He respected the American Indians and was not swayed by what he saw as "white greed."

During his last four years of military service, from 1844 to 1848, Taylor achieved stunning military success and great national fame. These successes led to his entry into the world of politics.

## The Army of Occupation

Taylor's political rise began in 1844, when he became commander of the First Military District at Fort Jesup, Louisiana. Many of the troops stationed at Fort Jesup were earmarked to serve if Mexico attacked the Republic of Texas. The United States wanted to annex the Republic and admit it to the United States. When Texas did become a state in 1845, a border dispute with Mexico developed. During this time Taylor moved his army of occupation into Texas, establishing a base of operations at Corpus Christi. Conditions were deplorable. There was no proper sanitation, and many men became ill with dysentery. Unseasonably cold weather also hampered the troops.

When diplomatic efforts eventually failed, the United States was ready to take control of the disputed territory. This was the beginning of the Mexican War.

## ▶ The Battles of Palo Alto
## and Resaca de la Palma

From Corpus Christi, Taylor was ordered to move his troops south to the Rio Grande, which Texas claimed as its southern border. On March 1, 1846, they headed south. By March 28, they had set up camp on the north bank of the Rio Grande, a half-mile from Matamoros, Mexico. This was a hundred miles south of the original boundary.

On May 8, Taylor's troops were outnumbered three to one when they engaged in the Battle of Palo Alto. The deadly artillery and cavalry battle killed ninety-two

▲ Many Mexican and American soldiers died at the Battle of Palo Alto, including Major Ringgold. This painting depicts his death.

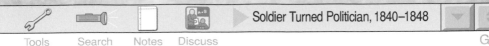

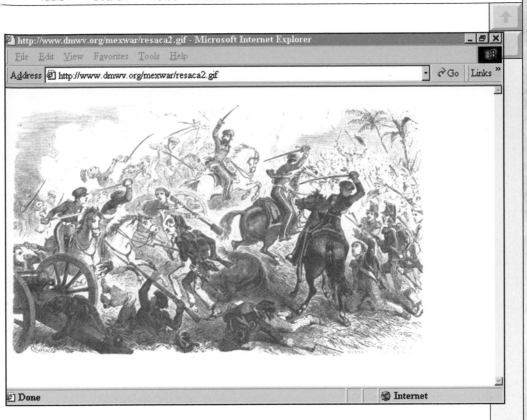

*This sketch illustrates a battle at Resaca de la Palma.*

Mexican soldiers and nine Americans. The Mexican forces retreated near sundown, when they ran out of ammunition for their cannons. Taylor's men had won the battle, but the Mexican force had not been defeated.

The next day Taylor pursued the enemy, which had fled south. That afternoon they encountered the Mexican forces at Resaca de la Palma, a shallow ravine that had once been part of the Rio Grande. Without ammunition for the artillery and without any food in over a day, the Mexican troops suffered from low morale. Nevertheless, the fierce two-hour battle included hand-to-hand conflict. Taylor was part of it, directing his men from a position on the battlefield. This was a risky undertaking but one that his

▲ *Zachary Taylor's troops endured the four-day Battle of Monterey.*

troops admired. Dealt a stunning defeat, the Mexican army fled. They had lost two hundred men. The Americans had lost forty-nine.

News of Old Rough and Ready's victories turned him into a national hero. President Polk sent Taylor a congratulatory letter that included a promotion to brevet major general. Congress passed a resolution thanking him, his officers, and his men "for the fortitude, skill, enterprise, and courage, which have distinguished the recent brilliant operations on the Rio Grande."[1] A gold medal was specially designed for him. The best reward was the one he received on June 18, 1846, when Congress made him a full major general, the highest military rank at that time.

## The Battles of Monterey and Buena Vista

Taylor was instructed to cross the Rio Grande into Mexico and take the important town of Monterey, 250 miles south of Matamoros. At the beginning of September 1846, Taylor and his troops began their campaign. They reached Monterey on September 19.

A four-day battle began the next day. Taylor's forces suffered heavy losses: 122 killed and 368 wounded. This may have been why he accepted a controversial peace treaty from the retreating Mexican army. Under its terms, the Mexican army headed south, and Taylor agreed not to fight

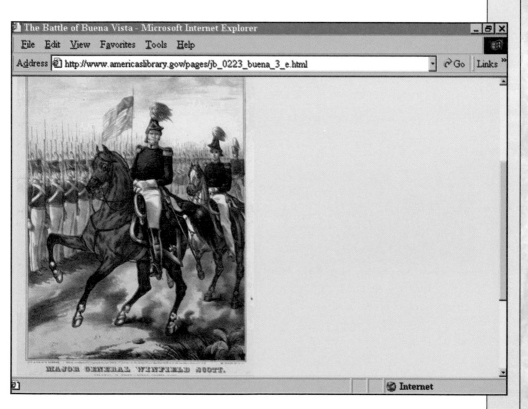

MAJOR GENERAL WINFIELD SCOTT.

▲ *When Taylor negotiated a peace treaty with the Mexican army, an angry President Polk reassigned his troops to Major General Winfield Scott.*

again for eight weeks. Unfortunately, President Polk and his advisors had concluded that war was the only way to bring about negotiations with Mexico. No one had communicated this to Taylor, though, so he signed the treaty.

President Polk was not pleased with the treaty or with Taylor. He sent the only member of the military with more seniority, General Winfield Scott, to Mexico to take command. Scott reassigned most of Taylor's troops to his command, and was not able to inform Taylor.

In February 1847, Taylor and 5,000 of his troops were near Saltillo, Mexico, surrounded by General Antonio López de Santa Anna's army of some 20,000 men. The

ANTONIO LÓPEZ DE SANTA ANNA: THE MAN AND HIS TIMES - Microsoft Internet Explorer

File   Edit   View   Favorites   Tools   Help

Address http://www.pbs.org/kera/usmexicanwar/dialogues/prelude/santa_anna/d6beng.html   Go   Links

**Antonio López de Santa Anna: A Man and His Times**
A conversation with Jesús Velasco-Márquez
Instituto Tecnol÷gico Aut÷nomo de MÚxico

**What kind of man was Santa Anna?**

Antonio López de Santa Anna was a complex figure not easily described in a few words. He was a man of great contradictions. On one hand, he was an extremely frivolous man, surprisingly trite and politically inconsistent. He was a wealthy man who had haciendas as defined by the standards of the period. But Santa Anna did not seek fortune but rather sought public acclaim and recognition more than money. He was a person who sought power more for the sake of its prestige than for its responsibility.

Santa Anna was a unique man and, according to memoirs of the time, was reportedly a handsome man. He did not

Done   Internet

*Santa Anna was a very powerful military leader who sought public recognition and acclaim more than money. His appreciation for Mexico led him to defend his country during the Mexican War.*

JUSTICE.              PEACE

UNION

*During the Battle of Buena Vista, Taylor showed great courage when he refused to leave his wounded soldiers behind. Yet Taylor was not alone when he showed this bravery. His faithful horse and animal companion, Old Whitey, was always with him.*

resulting Battle of Buena Vista involved infantry, cavalry, and artillery. It went on for two long days. Old Rough and Ready held his ground. When someone suggested that the American troops should retreat to a better position, Taylor replied, "No, we will decide the battle here! I will never, alive, leave my wounded behind."[2] Reportedly, he sat on his horse, Old Whitey, so close to the center of the battle that his aides asked him to take a safer position.

The Mexican army retreated; almost six hundred of their men had been killed. The Americans lost 272 men, including a large number of officers.

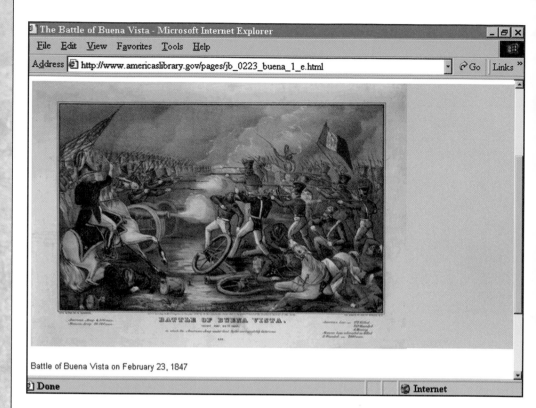

The Battle of Buena Vista - Microsoft Internet Explorer

File  Edit  View  Favorites  Tools  Help

Address http://www.americaslibrary.gov/pages/jb_0223_buena_1_e.html   Go  Links

Battle of Buena Vista on February 23, 1847

Done    Internet

*President Polk blamed Taylor for the unnecessary loss of American officers at the Battle of Buena Vista. But the American public thought otherwise. They believed that since the Mexican army had retreated, Taylor had gained headway to securing the territory for the United States.*

Again, President Polk was unhappy. He blamed Taylor for the enormous losses in an unnecessary battle. The American people thought otherwise. They felt Taylor had defeated a much larger enemy army. The Mexican War eventually ended in 1847, when General Scott invaded Mexico City.

## The Hero Becomes a Candidate

Eager to see his family after a two-and-a-half-year separation, Taylor was granted leave. He returned to Louisiana in December 1847. His first stop was New Orleans, where the

*Campaign banner from the*  *Election of 1848.*

crowd's joyous response overwhelmed him. When he moved on to New Orleans a few days later, the city honored him with a number of festivities, including a banquet and fireworks.

The nation was preparing to elect a new president, and Zachary Taylor had been mentioned as a possible candidate. A few politicians had spoken to him as early as 1846 about running for president. Taylor was not a political person at all, though. He had never even voted in an election. Still, he had no fondness for President Polk, and the promise of a political life sounded appealing after all of his rough-and-ready years in the military.

At its national convention in 1848, the Whig Party nominated Taylor as its presidential candidate. Millard Fillmore was chosen to run as his vice president. In the election, a three-way race against Lewis Cass (a Democrat) and former president Martin Van Buren (at the time a member of the Free Soil Party), Taylor won a narrow victory. He carried eight slave states and seven free states.

The successful soldier had become a politician. Zachary Taylor had become the twelfth president of the United States.

**Chapter 5 ▶**

# President Zachary Taylor, 1848–1850

**Z**achary Taylor was inaugurated on March 5, 1849. Although a bitterly cold wind blew that day, crowds still thronged the streets. President Polk and President-elect Taylor rode together in their carriage to Capitol Hill for the ceremony. They had met a number of times since the election, and Polk was not impressed with Taylor. He later wrote that Taylor was "uneducated, exceedingly ignorant

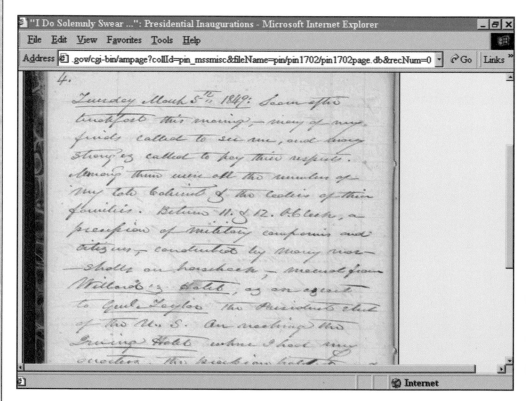

▲ Taylor's handwritten inaugural address.

of public affairs, and I should judge of very ordinary capacity,"[1] but many historians disagree.

Taylor enjoyed Washington. True to his nickname, he wore comfortable clothes and sometimes walked through the streets unconcerned about his safety. Still, he did not have an easy time as president. Many problems confronted him as he took office.

## Troubles of the Nation

American Indian attacks in Florida were causing panic among the settlers. The settlers wanted more troops sent to the area and asked that the militia be called up. Taylor was not spurred to action by the panic. As a commander, he had tried to be thorough and just. An investigation revealed that only five Seminoles were responsible for the trouble. Taylor sent some troops to Florida, but he refused to call up the militia. The matter was handled mostly by negotiations with emissaries for the Seminole people.

The nation was also afflicted with a serious outbreak of cholera that had begun in December 1848. From New York to Louisiana to Wisconsin, people were dying. More than five thousand people died in New York City alone. Roughly 10 percent of the total population of St. Louis died in the outbreak. The epidemic was so terrible that Taylor called for a day of prayer and remembrance of the victims, on Friday, August 3, 1849. He was not a religious person, but some critics saw his proclamation as a failure to separate church and state.

## The Issue of Slavery

The country also faced another crisis, one that divided its citizens and its states. Zachary Taylor had owned slaves all through his adult life, but he was not a vocal supporter of

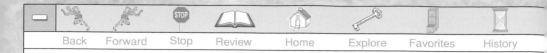

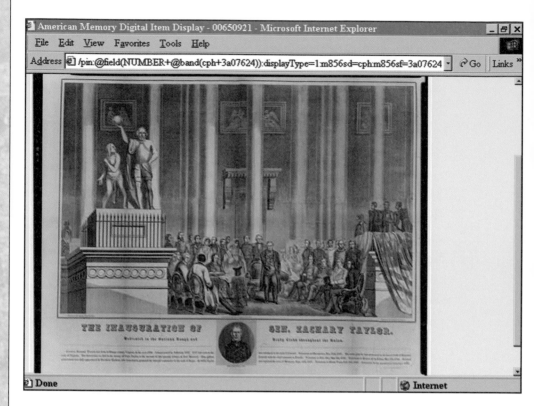

American Memory Digital Item Display - 00650921 - Microsoft Internet Explorer

File    Edit    View    Favorites    Tools    Help

Address /pin:@field(NUMBER+@band(cph+3a07624)):displayType=1:m856sd=cph:m856sf=3a07624    Go    Links

THE INAUGURATION OF    GEN. ZACHARY TAYLOR.

Done    Internet

Zachary Taylor faced many problems from the moment he assumed his role as president. These included a cholera epidemic and the ongoing issues of slavery and statehood.

slavery. This issue made matters difficult when, in 1849, two western territories, California and New Mexico, wished to become states. The nation wanted to know: Would these new states permit slavery, or would they be free states?

In the case of California, Taylor wished a speedy statehood. He was convinced that California would choose to be a free state. New Mexico had long been a slave-free part of Mexico. Now that it belonged to the United States, it could remain free on its way to statehood—unless Texas tried to annex it and impose slavery on it. Many New

Mexicans saw Texas as an enemy because of a bitter border dispute between the two territories.

Taylor's feelings were quite clear. He believed that any new states should be admitted as free states, but not everyone agreed. When California requested statehood, Congress seemed likely to approve. A Northern congressmen, David Wilmot, attached an amendment that prohibited slavery in California and in all the territories that the United States had acquired after the Mexican War. This became known as the Wilmot Proviso, and Taylor supported it. Slave states then threatened to vote against the statehood proposal.

## The Compromise of 1850

The statehood and other controversies regarding slavery led in January 1850 to the Compromise of 1850. As proposed by Senator Henry Clay, the compromise contained eight resolutions that tried to make amends to both free and slave states. For example, the resolutions called for California to make its own decision about slavery and suggested the abolishment of the slave trade (but not slavery itself) in the District of Columbia. On the other hand, one of the resolutions provided for a stronger fugitive slave law. Another part of the compromise clearly permitted slave trade between states. One resolution that particularly irked President Taylor called for "open territories" where slavery could still be an option. This was called popular sovereignty, the idea that citizens in the territories should vote to decide whether the territory should be slave or free.

Taylor was not pleased about the open territories provision or the other concessions proposed for slave states. His angry response to the proposal led three southern senators to suggest that southern states might secede from,

or leave, the Union. Taylor would not listen to such a suggestion and asked for changes in the resolutions.

A great debate took place during the first half of 1850. Interestingly, while Taylor continued to lobby for the admission of California and New Mexico as free states, he directed his son to buy another plantation with more slaves.[2] Taylor was not opposed to slavery, but he was unlike many slaveholders. He never sold a slave and made certain that they were well cared for. Records indicate that the slaves at Cypress Grove, another plantation that Taylor owned in Mississippi, received one pound of meat plus fresh milk each day. Taylor made sure that they also received enough vegetables and bread. He also gave each of his slaves as much as five dollars for Christmas.

As the summer of 1850 arrived, the debate over slave-holding in the new states remained deadlocked. Taylor refused to compromise.

## ▶ The Clayton-Bulwer Treaty

As the issue of compromise simmered, an international problem confronted Taylor.

Great Britain, which held colonies in Central America, wished to build a canal across Nicaragua to unite the Pacific and Atlantic Oceans. The United States also wanted to build such a canal. Britain seized a small island off the Pacific coast of Nicaragua, directly opposite one end of the proposed canal. President Taylor and his advisors saw this as a deliberate attempt by Britain

◀ *Secretary of State John M. Clayton.*

to gain control of the future canal. As a result, the United States and Britain negotiated the Clayton-Bulwer Treaty. It called for the two nations to renounce any claims on Central America and to protect any canal or cross-country railroad built across the isthmus.

Eventually, a canal was built in Panama instead. The Clayton-Bulwer Treaty was an important step that led to its building. It prevented Great Britain from expanding its interests in Central America.[3]

No one knows what else Taylor might have accomplished as president. He died four days after he signed the Clayton-Bulwer Treaty. He had served only sixteen months of his term.

**Chapter 6 ▶**

# Death and Legacy, 1850

The last healthy day of Zachary Taylor's life was Independence Day, 1850. He attended a Sunday school recital in the morning. That afternoon, in a ceremony at the new Washington Monument, he helped lay one of the cornerstones. Washington, D.C., was in the middle of a heat wave. The temperature was overpowering. By the time Taylor returned home that afternoon, he was hungry and thirsty. It may have led him to make a fatal mistake.

The cholera epidemic that had begun in late 1848 had continued. Washington newspapers sported headlines about the epidemic as it swept the capital. It was most likely caused by the unsanitary condition of the local water supply. The newspapers carried many suggestions. Residents were told to avoid eating raw fruits and vegetables or drinking milk and large quantities of water.

Independent to the end, Taylor ignored those warnings. He ate a few cherries and some raw vegetables. He also drank a great quantity of iced milk before dinner that night. By evening, he too had been stricken with cholera.

## ▶ The Death of the President

Doctors did not know much about cholera at the time, and the available medicines were not particularly helpful in treating it. He was prescribed opium and calomel (a compound of mercury then used as a laxative, but now considered dangerous). His doctors also bled him, believing that it would cleanse the disease from his body.

It just made Taylor weaker, though, and gave him severe blisters. Though he rallied enough on July 5 to sign the Clayton-Bulwer Treaty, his health declined over the next four days.

At 10:35 P.M. on July 9, he died. His last words are reported to have been: "I have always done my duty. I am ready to die. My only regret is for the friends I leave behind me."[1]

Taylor's death stunned the nation. His funeral procession was two miles long. His hearse was pulled by eight white horses, each handled by a groom wearing a white turban. Old Whitey, his favorite horse, followed the coffin all the way to the Congressional Cemetery.

Taylor was not buried in Washington, though. Instead, his body was transported to Kentucky. Sixteen weeks later he was interred in what is now called the Zachary Taylor National Cemetery, near Louisville.

By the time his body was laid to rest, the storm over slavery had seemed to calm down. The Compromise of 1850 had passed the House and Senate, despite the wishes of Zachary Taylor, and was approved by President Millard Fillmore.

## ▶ His Legacy

Historians have had a difficult time reaching conclusions about Taylor's short presidency. How would

*Although Zachary Taylor served* ▶ *just sixteen months of his four-year term; he accomplished much during his brief presidency. He is pictured here with his son-in-law Colonel William Bliss.*

history have been different if he had served his full term? Would the Compromise of 1850 have passed as it was, or would it have been changed first? Would those changes have had an impact on the war brewing over the slavery issue? Most of all, historians have wondered what kind of president Zachary Taylor would have been.

In a letter to the British foreign minister, Sir Henry Bulwer, the English diplomat who had helped negotiate the Clayton-Bulwer Treaty, wrote, "His intentions were always good; his word could always be relied upon; his manners were downright, simple, straightforward; his name was popular throughout the Union, and he died almost universally respected and lamented."[2]

Perhaps newspaper editor Horace Greeley described Taylor best when he wrote in the *New York Tribune* on July 10, 1850, "A Southern man and a slaveholder, his mind was above the narrow prejudices of district and class and steadily aimed at the good of the nation as a whole."[3]

## Chapter Notes

### Chapter 1. Old Rough and Ready, September 1812

1. A. C. Duddleston, "Fort Harrison in History," *Magazine of American History*, Vol. 28, 1892, p. 22.

2. Silas Bent McKinley and Silas Bent, *Old Rough and Ready: The Life and Times of Zachary Taylor* (New York: Vanguard, 1946), p. 47.

### Chapter 2. Taylor's Early Years, 1784–1815

1. Holman Hamilton, *Zachary Taylor: Soldier of the Republic* (Indianapolis, Ind.: Bobbs-Merrill, 1941), facing p. 136.

2. Elbert B. Smith, *The Presidencies of Zachary Taylor and Millard Fillmore* (Lawrence: University Press of Kansas, 1988), p. 27.

### Chapter 3. Distinguished Soldier, 1816–1840

1. K. Jack Bauer, *Zachary Taylor: Soldier, Planter, Statesman of the Old Southwest* (Baton Rouge: Louisiana State University Press, 1985), p. 29.

2. Holman Hamilton, *Zachary Taylor: Soldier of the Republic* (Indianapolis, Ind.: Bobbs-Merrill, 1941), p. 69.

3. Bauer, pp. 104–105.

4. Hamilton, p. 101.

5. Ibid., p. 108.

6. Bauer, p. 82.

7. Brainerd Dyer, *Zachary Taylor* (Baton Rouge: Louisiana State University Press, 1946), pp. 109–110.

8. Ibid., p. 110.

9. Otto B. Engelmann, "The Second Illinois in the Mexican War," *Journal of the Illinois State Historical Society*, Vol. XXVI No. 4, Jan. 1934, p. 438.

## Chapter 4. Soldier Turned Politician, 1840–1848

1. Brainerd Dyer, *Zachary Taylor* (Baton Rouge: Louisiana State University Press, 1946), p. 179.

2. Ibid., p. 235.

## Chapter 5. President Zachary Taylor, 1849–1850

1. K. Jack Bauer, *Zachary Taylor: Soldier, Planter, Statesman of the Old Southwest* (Baton Rouge: Louisiana University Press, 1985), p. 257.

2. Elbert B. Smith, *The Presidencies of Zachary Taylor and Millard Fillmore* (Lawrence: University Press of Kansas, 1988), p. 122.

3. Ibid., pp. 84–85.

## Chapter 6. Death and Legacy, 1850

1. K. Jack Bauer, *Zachary Taylor: Soldier, Planter, Statesman of the Old Southwest* (Baton Rouge: Louisiana University Press, 1985), p. 316.

2. Holman Hamilton, *Zachary Taylor: Soldier in the White House* (Indianapolis, Ind.: Bobbs-Merrill, 1951), p. 412.

3. Elbert B. Smith, *The Presidencies of Zachary Taylor and Millard Fillmore* (Lawrence: University Press of Kansas, 1988), p. 158.

## Further Reading

Bauer, K. Jack. *Zachary Taylor: Soldier, Planter, Statesman of the Old Southwest.* Baton Rouge: Louisiana State University Press, 1993.

Brunelli, Carol. *Zachary Taylor.* Chanhassen, Mich.: Child's World, 2001.

Collins, David R. *Zachary Taylor: 12th President of the United States.* Ada, Okla.: Garrett Educational Corporation, 1989.

Joseph, Paul. *Zachary Taylor.* Edina, Minn.: ABDO Publishing, 1999.

Kent, Zachary. *Zachary Taylor.* Chicago: Children's Press, 1988.

Martin, Patricia M. *Zachary Taylor.* New York: Putnam, 1969.

Mills, Bronwyn. *The Mexican War.* New York: Facts on File, 1992.

Nardo, Don. *The Mexican-American War.* San Diego, Calif.: Lucent Books, 1999.

Smith, Elbert B. *The Presidencies of Zachary Taylor & Millard Fillmore.* Lawrence: University Press of Kansas, 1988.

Todd, Anne. *The War of 1812.* Mankato, Minn.: Capstone Press, Inc., 2000.

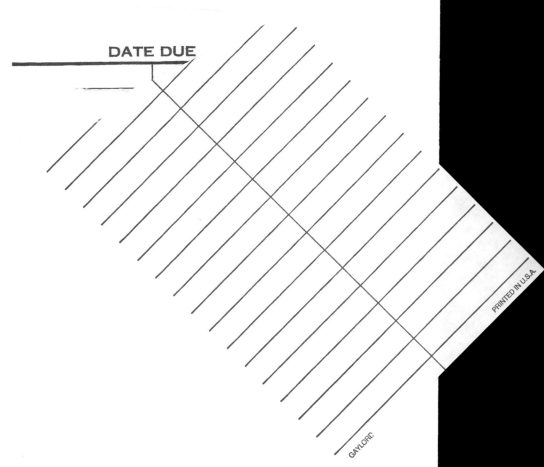

DATE DUE

GAYLORD

PRINTED IN U.S.A.